Pebble® Plus

Spokes

BIKE SAFETY
A Crash Course
BY LISA J. AMSTUTZ

raintree
a Capstone company — publishers for children

Raintree is an imprint of Capstone Global Library Limited, a company incorporated in England and Wales having its registered office at 264 Banbury Road, Oxford, OX2 7DY – Registered company number: 6695582

www.raintree.co.uk
myorders@raintree.co.uk

Edited by Jeni Wittrock
Designed by Kyle Grenz
Production by Jennifer Walker
Picture research by Sarah Schuette
Photo Schedule by Marcy Morin
Production by Capstone Global Library Ltd
Printed and bound in China

ISBN 978 1 4747 3370 0
20 19 18 17 16
10 9 8 7 6 5 4 3 2 1

British Library Cataloguing in Publication Data
A full catalogue record for this book is available from the British Library.

Acknowledgements
We would like to thank the following for permission to reproduce photographs: Capstone Studio: Karon Dubke, 5, 7, 9; Corbis: Mika, 15; Glow Images: All Canada Photos/Henry Georgi, 17, Bridge/Corbis/Holger Winkler/A.B., 11; Shutterstock: chirayusarts, 19, Monkey Business Images, 21, spotmatik, cover, 13

Design Elements
Shutterstock: filip robert, Kalmatsuy Tatyana

We would like to thank Gail Saunders-Smith for her invaluable help in the preparation of this book.

Every effort has been made to contact copyright holders of material reproduced in this book. Any omissions will be rectified in subsequent printings if notice is given to the publisher.

All the internet addresses (URLs) given in this book were valid at the time of going to press. However, due to the dynamic nature of the internet, some addresses may have changed, or sites may have changed or ceased to exist since publication. While the author and publisher regret any inconvenience this may cause readers, no responsibility for any such changes can be accepted by either the author or the publisher.

Contents

Safety first

It's a perfect day for
a bike ride. The sun is out
and your friends are ready
to roll. But wait!
Think about safety first.

What to wear

Bikers need the right gear.

A helmet protects your head.

Fasten the strap snugly

under your chin.

What you wear is important.

Bright colours make it easy to

be seen. Avoid loose clothing.

It might get caught in the

bike chain. Tie shoelaces tight.

Safety check

If your bike isn't working properly, it's not safe to ride. Always test your brakes. They should stop the wheels from turning. The tyres should feel firm.

It's important to sit comfortably on your bike. Make sure your feet touch the pedals. The handlebars should be easy to reach.

Use your head

Cycle tracks and cycle lanes are safe places to ride. Need to cross the street? Hop off your bike and walk across at a crossing. Look both ways first.

When you ride, pay attention. Don't talk on a mobile phone or wear headphones. Keep your hands on the handlebars and your feet on the pedals.

Stay safe

Beep! Avoid getting in a crash. A horn or bell lets others know you are near. Use hand signals to show where you are heading.

left turn   stop/slow down   right turn

19

Tell an adult where you
are cycling. Someone might
need to find you. Always
cycle home before dark.
Have fun and ride safely!

Glossary

brake tool that slows down or stops a bike

crossing place where people can safely cross the street

handlebar part of a bicycle that the rider holds on to and uses to steer

hand signal special sign to show others that you plan to stop or turn

helmet hard hat that protects the head

Read more

Being Safe on a Bike (Keep Yourself Safe), Honor Head (Franklin Watts, 2015)

Cycling (Beginners Plus), Hazel Maskell (Usborne Publishing, 2015)

Should Henry Wear a Helmet? (Staying Safe), Rebecca Rissman (Raintree, 2014)

Websites

www.crucial-crew.org/interactive-safety-game/cycling-safety.cfm
This interactive game shows the important things to think about when cycling.

talesoftheroad.direct.gov.uk/cycling-safety.php
Learn about bike safety with this fun, interactive website.

Index